ADDING
FIRST MATH

KidHaven PUBLISHING

By Brenda McHale

Published in 2022 by
KidHaven Publishing, an Imprint of Greenhaven Publishing, LLC
29 East 21st Street
New York, NY 10010

© 2022 Booklife Publishing
This edition is published by arrangement with Booklife Publishing

All rights reserved. No part of this book may be reproduced in any form without permission in writing from the publisher, except by a reviewer.

Edited by: Robin Twiddy
Designed by: Lydia Wiliams

Find us on

Cataloging-in-Publication Data

Names: McHale, Brenda.
Title: Adding / Brenda McHale.
Description: New York : KidHaven Publishing, 2022. | Series: First math |
Identifiers: ISBN 9781534538849 (pbk.) | ISBN 9781534538863 (library bound) | ISBN 9781534538856 (6 pack) | ISBN 9781534538870 (ebook)
Subjects: LCSH: Addition--Juvenile literature. | Arithmetic--Juvenile literature.
Classification: LCC QA115.M343 2022 | DDC 513.2'11--dc23

Printed in the United States of America

CPSIA compliance information: Batch #BSKH22: For further information contact Greenhaven Publishing LLC, New York, New York at 1-844-317-7404.

Please visit our website, www.greenhavenpublishing.com. For a free color catalog of all our high-quality books, call toll free 1-844-317-7404 or fax 1-844-317-7405.

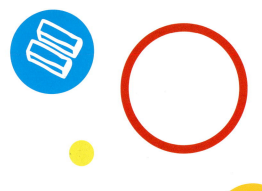
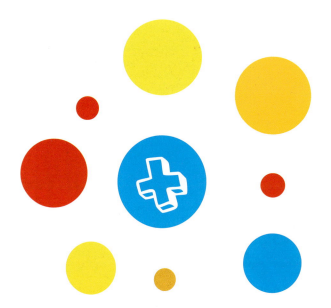
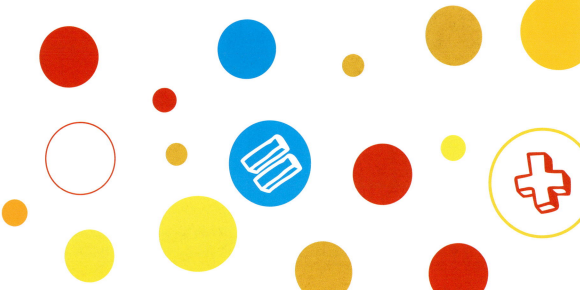

PHOTO CREDITS

Front cover – Gladskikh Tatiana ml – suns07butterfly mr – taviphoto. 4 – Oksana Kuzmina. 5 – Jakub Krechowicz. 6 – Ben Schonewille. 7 – GrashAlex. 8 – Hong Vo, Alted Studio, Diana Taliun. 9 – Marta Korowaj. 10 – hramovnick. 11 – Maya Kruchankova. 12 & 13 – chonlasub woravichan, bluehand, Steven Russell Smith Ohio, Vangert, southmind. 14 & 15 – fame kittituch, prozaika119. 16 – amlet, Roman Samokhin. 17 – loskutnikov. 18 & 19 – stockphoto-gra, FocusStocker f. 20 – Mr Aesthetics. 21 – New Africa. 22 – koosen. 23 – bergamont, Mr Aesthetics, New Africa, bergamont. 24 – Sharomka, Tim UR, Rodica Ciorba.

Images are courtesy of Shutterstock.com. With thanks to Getty Images, Thinkstock Photo, and iStockphoto.

CONTENTS

PAGE 4 — What Is Adding?
PAGE 6 — Can You Count?
PAGE 8 — All Together
PAGE 10 — What Are + and =?
PAGE 12 — Start Adding
PAGE 14 — Count the Cars
PAGE 16 — Add the Apples
PAGE 18 — Numbers
PAGE 20 — How Many?
PAGE 22 — Add Your Numbers
PAGE 24 — Adding Fun

WHAT IS ADDING?

Blocks are good for adding.

Adding means putting things together.
You can add numbers or things.

1 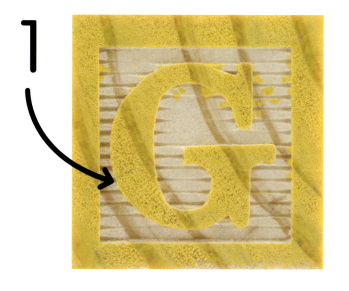 1

1 and 1 become 2 when they are added together.

  2

The new number is bigger than the numbers you added.

CAN YOU COUNT?

Count them slowly.

Can you count these baby ducks? Did you count to 9?

See how 1 bead is added each time.

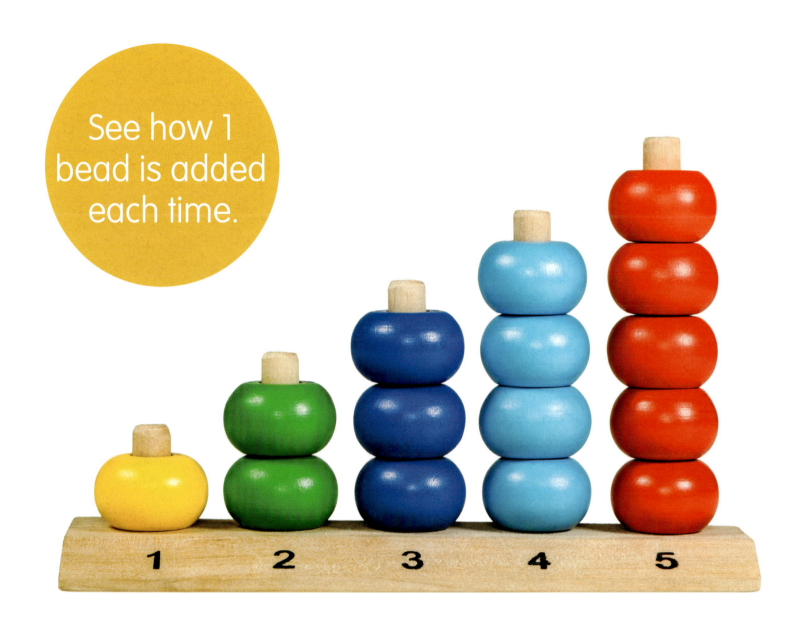

Counting is like adding 1 each time.

ALL TOGETHER

3 eggs

4 eggs

The new number is how many things there are altogether.

There are 7 eggs in the basket altogether.

Adding them together is like putting them all into the same basket.

WHAT ARE + AND =?

This is called a plus sign.

If you see a cross like this +, it tells you to add the two things on either side of it.

This is an equals sign.
It can tell us what something adds up to.

START ADDING

There are 3 fish and 2 fish.
Let's put them together!

Altogether there are 5.
3 + 2 = 5.

COUNT THE CARS

Count carefully.

Here are some toy cars to count.

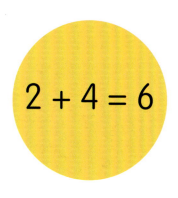

$2 + 4 = 6$

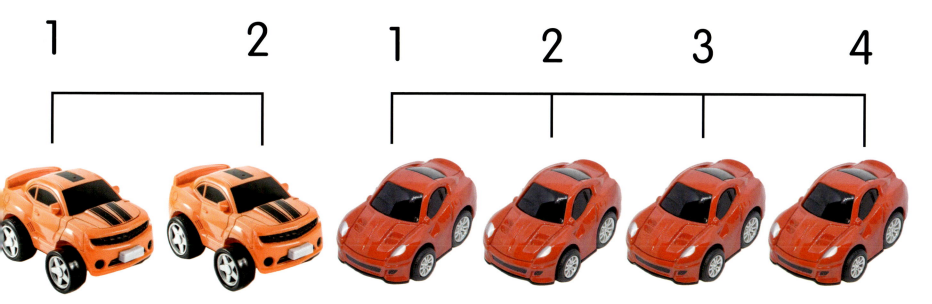

How many are there altogether?
Did you count 6?

ADD THE APPLES

2 + 2 = 4

Here are 2 apples and 2 more apples. There are 4 apples.

There are 4 apples here too!

NUMBERS

Count each group of balls.
How many are in each group?

Adding the groups together and counting all the balls gives us the same answer: 8!

HOW MANY?

Add the dots together.

Do you like to play dominoes?
You count dots when you play dominoes.

$$5 + 2 = 7$$

When you add numbers together,
the total is called a sum.

ADD YOUR NUMBERS

4 + 4 =

a) 8
b) 10
c) 5

Answer: a) 8

What number should go in the box?

These all have the same total.
Do you know what it is?

Answer: 7